THE DOGS IN DICKENS
BY
CUMBERLAND CLARK

BOOKS BY CUMBERLAND CLARK

1. DICKENS' LETTER TO COLBOURN. Relating to the controversy occasioned by the contribution of Walter Savage Landor to Pic-Nic Papers. With facsimile letter.
2. DICKENS AND HIS JEWISH CHARACTERS. Gives the correspondence between Dickens and Mrs. Davis relating to the character of Fagin.
3. SHAKESPEARE AND DICKENS. A Lecture on the plan of Plutarch's parallel lives.
4. DICKENS' LETTERS TO CLARKSON STANFIELD. Being the story of their great friendship. With seven letters.
5. DICKENS AND THE YORKSHIRE SCHOOLS. With his letter to Mrs. S. C. Hall. An important letter which deals with his expedition to Yorkshire, and the origin of Squeers and Smike. With letter in facsimile.
6. DICKENS AND TALFOURD. With an address and three unpublished letters to Talfourd, the father of the first Copyright Act, which put an end to the piracy of Dickens' writings.
7. DICKENS AND DEMOCRACY. With publication of his original manuscript on the Working Classes, together with his original letter to Dr. Southwood Smith on "The Condition of the Poor."
8. THE GREAT WAR CELEBRATED IN SONG. A book of war songs, set to music.
9. ASTRONOMY IN THE POETS. The first half of this book is a treatise on Astronomy in Shakespeare.
10. THE MERRY SONG BOOK. With 100 merry songs.
11. THE GOLDEN SONG BOOK. With 200 songs.
12. THE CONCERT PARTY ALBUM. Ten comedy songs, with music.
13. THE EMPIRE SONG BOOK. With 200 songs.
14. THE FLOWER FAIRIES. A Musical Fairy Play for Children.
15. DICKENS AND THE BEGGING-LETTER WRITER. With publication of a Dickens' autograph letter.
16. DICKENS' LONDON. A Lecture on Charles Dickens' life in London, the houses he lived in, and the London scenes and characters he described in his books.
17. BRITAIN OVERSEAS. The story of the foundation and development of the British Empire.
18. IN PRAISE OF LOVE. Six romance songs, with music.
19. LECTURES ON BYRON'S LIFE AND WORKS.
20. ENGLAND'S FIGHT AGAINST COMMUNISM.
21. A STUDY OF SHAKESPEARE'S MACBETH.

THE DOGS IN DICKENS

BY

CUMBERLAND CLARK

COPYRIGHT

HASKELL HOUSE PUBLISHERS LTD.
Publishers of Scarce Scholarly Books
NEW YORK, N. Y. 10012
1973

HASKELL HOUSE PUBLISHERS LTD.
Publishers of Scarce Scholarly Books
280 LAFAYETTE STREET
NEW YORK, N. Y. 10012

Library of Congress Cataloging in Publication Data

Clark, Cumberland, 1862-
　The dogs in Dickens.

　Reprint of the 1926 ed. privately printed at the Chiswick Press, London.
　1. Dickens, Charles, 1812-1870. 2. Dogs in literature. I. Title.
PR4592.D6C55　1973　　　　823'.8　　　　73-9642
ISBN 0-8383-1713-8

Printed in the United States of America

CONTENTS

	PAGE
INTRODUCTION	7
BULL'S-EYE	11
DIOGENES	19
BOXER	29
JIP	34
MERRYLEGS	47
POODLES	51
SPORTING DOGS AND OTHERS . . .	55
PONTO	57
BLOODHOUNDS	59
VARIOUS DOGS	62

THE DOGS IN DICKENS

FROM THE LARGE HEART OF Dickens flowed a swelling stream of sympathy and understanding which embraced all his fellow inhabitants of the Earth. It was not only into sorrows that he entered with all the greatness of his soul, helping, encouraging, and soothing. He could share in the joys of others with equal perception and insight, and feel them as if they were his own. His sympathetic character may appeal to us more when he is describing the pathetic death of Little Nell, the pitiful case of Caleb Plummer's blind daughter, the harrowing experiences of little Oliver, the miseries of the scholars at Dotheboys Hall, and the hundred other cases in which sickness, poverty, distress, or hardship are paraded before us to awaken our

Christianity. But sympathy is not the companion of sorrow alone. It is just as much the friend of joy, and only because it appears more necessary to sorrow than to joy do we seem to grow nearer to the soul of the great novelist in tears than in laughter. Nothing, however, could be more real than the sympathy of Dickens with happiness. Whether we take the beautiful love scenes from "Martin Chuzzlewit," "David Copperfield," "Little Dorrit," and other books, or whether we read of Mr. Fezziwig's ball, the Cratchits' Christmas dinner, the visit of Kit and his family to Astleys, and many other happy incidents that occur to the mind, we see the real humanitarian, the one who sympathizes with all sides, not one alone, of human experience.

With a sympathy that was so universal it is natural to find Dickens strongly moved by cases of helplessness and limitation. Little children best illustrate this trait, for they are handled with the greatest love and tender care. However, his sympathies, great as they were, were not bounded by humanity, but extended beyond the world of men and women into the animal kingdom. His love for dumb creatures is evidenced by instance after instance in his books. There is Grip, the raven, and Whisker, Mr. Garland's amusing pony; but the author's love of animals is best illustrated in his dogs. There could be no better way, then, to appreciate and understand this side of Dickens than to collect the stories of his dogs and pass them in review. It is not necessary to take every occasion on which a dog is mentioned, for the mention is often incidental and refers more to the human character than the animal, but there are certain dogs in the works of the novelist which he has endowed with a strong personality of their own, and which are as important to the action of the story as many of the men and women. For example, in "Little Dorrit" the dog Lion is introduced to emphasize an unpleasant side of Mr. Henry Gowan's character. The Dorrit sisters enter the artist's studio in Venice when making a call upon the Gowans, and there discover Blandois posing for a picture. Lion has taken an instinctive dislike to this villainous man and growls at him menacingly in reply to his provoking glances. Little Dorrit calls Gowan's attention to the fact that the animal is about to spring at his enemy, and the artist flings down his brush and treats Lion with the utmost brutality and cruelty. The dark side of Minnie's unworthy husband is thus revealed to Little Dorrit, and the dog, having served this purpose, disappears from the narrative. Lion is not of great help, therefore, in arriving at Dickens attitude towards dumb animals, but the position is quite the reverse when we come to consider such important canine characters as Bull's-eye, Diogenes, Boxer, Jip, Poodles, and Merrylegs.

In telling the stories of the dogs of Dickens, not only will his kindness towards our dumb friends be shown, but it will be found that his knowledge of them was extensive. This he gained in the same way as his knowledge of human beings, namely, by his wonderful powers of observation. He marvelled at the extraordinary instinct which dogs possess, he was astonished at their sagacity, he admired their great loyalty and faithfulness to their masters and mistresses, he saw how as pets they were often instrumental in arousing the finer feelings in men and women, he realized what they brought to human beings in the way of consolation and companionship, and knew that they brightened many a domestic hearth. Some of the scenes in which the dogs appear are among the most pathetic in the works, while others would not be so joyful without the presence of the dumb friend.

The dogs are necessary to the effect which the author set himself to attain and are often responsible for determining the course of events. From a study of the dogs, therefore, we may hope to broaden our knowledge of the real Dickens and appreciate better those qualities of insight, sympathy, and understanding, which made him great.

BULL'S-EYE

Perhaps the best known of Dickens' dogs is Bull's-eye, the companion of Bill Sikes, in "Oliver Twist." On his first introduction he is described as skulking into the room after his master, "a white shaggy dog, with his face scratched and torn in twenty different places." It cannot be said for Bull's-eye that he was a very lovable dog or the possessor of the more amiable traits that are often found in canine character. He was prone to "a certain malicious licking of the lips" and seemed to be "meditating an attack upon the legs of the first gentleman or lady he might encounter in the streets when he went out." On behalf of Bull's-eye it must be said that he was set a very bad example in the display of temper by Sikes, and was subjected to harsh and cruel treatment calculated to arouse the savage part in any animal. No doubt his master's enmity against mankind found a sympathetic response in Bull's-eye's habit of indulging in fierce conflicts with other dogs. Being a painful sufferer from brutality himself, he gave as good as he received, which is the nature of dumb animals. Treat them with kindness and they will respond; be cruel and unjust to them and they will be fierce and suspicious.

Bull's-eye was forced to stand much from Bill Sikes. In the parlour of a low public-house in Saffron Hill the housebreaker kicked and cursed his companion to relieve his own gloomy feelings, and Bull's-eye fixed his teeth in his boot. Dickens says truthfully, "dogs are not generally apt to revenge injuries inflicted upon them by their masters," but Bull's-eye's case was an exceptional one, as may be gathered from what followed his retaliation. Sikes seized the poker and opened a large clasp knife which he took from his pocket. He then ordered the dog to him for the purpose of cutting his throat. But Bull's-eye was too wise to walk calmly to the slaughter and stayed where he was and growled. Sikes, roused to fury, snatched the poker and began to assail the beast with savage blows. It would have gone hard with Bull's-eye but for the timely entrance of Fagin who, opening the door, gave him the chance of escape from the mad fury of the robber. He hid in the back yard, only shrinking out when his tormentor had disappeared.

The chief quality of Bull's-eye is his sagacity. The above incident shows a complete knowledge of his master's intentions, and if these appeared somewhat obvious in this case, there were others in which they were less plain. When Oliver was recaptured by the gang while performing a commission for Mr. Brownlow, Bull's-eye played an important part in the proceedings. He was told to guard Oliver, and his fierce growling struck terror into the boy's heart. Bull's-eye showed a tendency to make sure that the captive did not escape by "attaching himself to his windpipe without delay," and only when they neared Fagin's hovel did he relax his vigilance, realizing that it was no longer so necessary. When Oliver made his desperate effort to escape, Nancy understood that Bull's-eye would thoroughly understand the position and perform his duty only too well.

"'Keep back the dog, Bill!' cried Nancy, springing before the door and closing it, as the

Jew and his two pupils darted out in pursuit; 'keep back the dog; he'll tear the boy to pieces.'

"'Serve him right!' cried Sikes, struggling to disengage himself from the girl's grasp. 'Stand off from me, or I'll split your head against the wall.'

"'I don't care for that, Bill; I don't care for that,' screamed the girl, struggling violently with the man: 'the child shan't be torn by the dog, unless you kill me first.'

"'Shan't he!' said Sikes, setting his teeth fiercely. 'I'll soon do that, if you don't keep off.'"

Nancy's intervention saved Oliver from the teeth of Bull's-eye, for just as Sikes flung the girl from him, Fagin and the boys returned with the unhappy captive.

The dog was acquainted with his master's friends and knew those who were safe and those who needed to be watched. He was on the alert when Fagin entered clad in an unfamiliar overcoat, but on Sikes saying: "Don't you know the devil when he's got a greatcoat on?" he went to his corner wagging his tail, "to show that he was as well satisfied as it was in his nature to be." But during Sikes' illness Bull's-eye saw little of anybody except the faithful Nancy, who attended the sick housebreaker. The latter complained bitterly of the manner in which Fagin and his accomplices had deserted him and was only mollified by the good things they brought with them when at last they did come to see him. This interest in the good things was shared by Bull's-eye, who caused Master Bates to exclaim: "I never see such a jolly dog as that. Smelling the grub like an old lady a-going to market! He'd make his fortun' on the stage that dog would, and rewive the drayma besides."

When Sikes had committed the foul murder of Nancy and left the horrible room where "the very feet of the dog were bloody," Bull's-eye became a fugitive with his guilty master. He toiled with him through Islington, Highgate, Hampstead Heath, Hendon, and back again, until he was "limping and lame from the unaccustomed exercise." But Bull's-eye's fidelity was an embarrassment and danger to Sikes in his flight from justice. It was a clue which might lead to his being traced and apprehended. The murderer resolved, therefore, to crown his long ill-treatment of the shaggy creature by destroying him.

"The dog, though—if any descriptions of him

were out, it would not be forgotten that the dog was missing, and had probably gone with him. This might lead to his apprehension as he passed along the streets. He resolved to drown him, and walked on, looking about for a pond, picking up a heavy stone and tying it to his handkerchief as he went.

"The animal looked up into his master's face while these preparations were making; and, whether his instinct apprehended something of their purpose, or the robber's side-long look at him was sterner than ordinary, skulked a little farther in the rear than usual, and cowered as he came slowly along. When his master halted at the brink of the pool, and looked round to call him, he stopped outright.

"'Do you hear me call? Come here!' cried Sikes.

"The animal came from the very force of habit, but as Sikes stooped to attach the handkerchief to his throat, he uttered a low growl and started back.

"'Come back!' said the robber, stamping on the ground.

"The dog wagged his tail, but moved not. Sikes made a running noose and called him again.

"The dog advanced, retreated, paused an instant, turned, and scoured away at his hardest speed.

"The man whistled again and again and sat down in the expectation that he would return. But no dog appeared, and at length he resumed his journey."

Bull's-eye's instinct and sagacity had saved his life, for he had again read aright his cruel master's intention. Frightened to remain with Sikes, the dog, guided again by his instinct, made his way to his old London haunts. Going round to the various places that he knew and finding them occupied by strangers—for Fagin and most of his accomplices had now been arrested—Bull's-eye came at length to the house in Jacob's Island, where Toby Crackit, Mr. Chitling, and a robber of fifty years were in hiding. When the dog jumped through a window and bounded into the room, he caused the greatest consternation to the company, for they feared that Sikes himself was near. In a little while they were more reassured and gave some water to Bull's-eye, who had run himself faint and lay panting on the ground.

"'He's drunk it all up, every drop,' said Chitling, after watching the dog some time in silence. 'Covered with mud—lame—half-blind—he must have come a long way.'"

While Bull's-eye curled himself up and fell into

the sleep of exhaustion, the men discussed what could have happened to Sikes. The theory of suicide is suggested, but their questionings are answered by the dreaded arrival of the murderer himself. Bull's-eye is alert on the instant and "ran whining to the door." Sikes enters and is surprised to see his dog there. He is told that he arrived alone some three hours before him.

Sikes' end is near. The police arrive at the house, and an infuriated crowd besiege the building. He resolves upon a desperate effort to escape by jumping into the Folly Ditch. He uses a rope which he fastens to the chimney and makes a noose to slip under his shoulders and so lower himself to within safe jumping distance of the ground. He has just put the noose over his head when he looks up and believes he sees the staring eyes of the dead Nancy, which have haunted him since his dastardly crime. He gives a shriek and falls. The noose draws tight, and he is hanged. But the eyes were not the creation of his imagination, for the following paragraph ends the great chapter:

"A dog, which had lain concealed till now, ran backwards and forwards on the parapet with a dismal howl, and, collecting himself for a spring, jumped for the dead man's shoulders. Missing his aim, he fell into the ditch, turning completely over as he went; and striking his head against a stone, dashed out his brains."

Thus was Bull's-eye instrumental in bringing justice and a fitting end upon the wicked Sikes, and followed his master even into the death valley. As a specimen of canine nature he had grave faults, but they were faults that were largely the result of his terrible environment and the cruel treatment he received. Dickens was always discussing the effect of environment on human beings, and no doubt believed that it had its effect in a lesser degree on animals also, which is true. When we recall the sureness of Bull's-eye's instinct, his wonderful sagacity, his ability to understand human thoughts, and his faithfulness to his ferocious master, even in death, we can imagine that he would have made a splendid companion and helper under different treatment and in different circumstances.

DIOGENES

Diogenes is one of the humorous characters in "Dombey and Son," and while he is not renowned for his cleverness, his real affection for Florence Dombey is a bright ray in the girl's lonely life in the gloomy house of her proud father.

Diogenes' original home was Doctor Blimber's School at Brighton, where little Paul Dombey was sent to be crammed with knowledge under the master's forcing system of education. Little notice had been taken of the dog before the child's arrival, but in Paul he found a friend, the first whom he accepted into his confidence. When the boy left the school, on account of the illness that could only end in the termination of the young life, he made a special request that Diogenes should be treated kindly. Dr. Blimber promised that he should have every care, but it does not appear that this was very faithfully carried out, for when an opportunity came to get rid of the animal, the schoolmaster was pleased enough to take it.

The opportunity was provided by Mr. Toots, a former schoolfellow of little Paul, who had now left the academy. He suffered from a hopeless attachment to Florence, and, on her brother's death, the kind thought occurred to him that she would probably like to have as a pet the dog of which the boy was so fond. Accordingly, he made arrangements for his removal, and having ensnared him into a hackney carriage, "on a false pretence of rats among the straw," brought him to the Dombey home. Mr. Toots has to apologize for the fact that Diogenes "ain't a lady's dog, you know," but hopes Florence will overlook that. Florence is very ready to do so and is truly grateful to the young man for his thoughtfulness.

If it had not been for the association with little Paul, Mr. Toots would doubtless have chosen some other animal to present to the lady of his heart, for we read:

"Though Diogenes was as ridiculous a dog as one would meet with on a summer's day; a blundering, ill-favoured, clumsy, bullet-headed dog, continually acting on a wrong idea that there was an enemy in the neighbourhood, whom it was meritorious to bark at; and though he was far from good-tempered, and certainly was not clever, and had hair all over his eyes, and a comic nose, and an inconsistent tail, and a gruff voice; he was dearer to Florence . . . than the most valuable and beautiful of his kind."

Mr. Toots was delighted with the grateful thanks of Florence, but Diogenes never appeared to bear him the goodwill that he deserved for the introduction to his kind mistress. On the other hand, he precipitated his exits by short runs at his legs with his mouth open, which, considering Mr. Toots' great anxiety concerning his garments, were extremely effective in getting rid of him. To Florence's overtures for love and friendship Diogenes responded from the first.

"And Di, the rough and gruff, as if his hairy hide were pervious to the tear that dropped upon it, and his dog's heart melted as it fell, put his nose up to her face, and swore fidelity."

Di, as Florence called him, drove some of the dulness from the girl's life, neglected as she was by her haughty parent. He constituted himself her companion and protector, and would lie for hours "looking lazily at her, upside down, out of the tops of his eyes, until from winking and winking he fell asleep." He made a friend and won the esteem of Susan Nipper, Florence's maid, in spite of her nervousness of dogs, for she realized how much her mistress valued him. On one occasion when Mr. Toots called, whose limited conversational powers were helped by the chance of asking how the dog was, Diogenes intervened at an unfortunate moment. Instead of making a precipitate departure, as usual, after leaving his cards, Mr.

Toots was reckless this time and kissed Susan on the cheek. Susan was surprised and amused and gave the young man a sharp push. Diogenes was watching through the banisters, and disapproving of the whole business made a dash at Toots, who only escaped with severe damage to his smart clothing.

Diogenes was also hostile to Mr. Carker, the manager of Dombey and Son, and well he might be, for the man's nefarious schemes boded no good for the household. Unfortunately, he was not a discriminating dog, and when Edith, the new Mrs. Dombey, first commenced to become intimate with his mistress, he objected to this intruder into their privacy and uttered a growling protest.

"But . . . he soon appeared to comprehend, that with the most amiable intentions, he had made one of those mistakes which will occasionally arise in the best regulated dog's life."

It was to Edith before her wedding that Florence confided how lonely she was and how grateful for the companionship of Diogenes. "Di and I pass whole days together sometimes," she said; and whole weeks and months would not have been an exaggeration. Her books and her music were her only other companions apart from the excellent Susan Nipper. Diogenes would generally lie quiet and placid, look out of the window, bark at a passing dog, but sometimes that supposed enemy in the neighbourhood would worry him and he would rush to the door—

> "whence, after a deafening disturbance, he would come jogging back with a ridiculous complacency that belonged to him, and . . . with the air of a dog who had done a public service."

Florence takes Diogenes with her on her visit to Brighton, whither she is followed surreptitiously by the doting Mr. Toots. The enamoured young man arranges to meet the object of his affection as if by accident, and affects the greatest surprise at seeing her, which hides his cunning from Florence. Diogenes, however, is suspicious and makes for Mr. Toots with his usual energy. His mistress reproves him and reminds him of their gratitude to the gentleman for bringing them together. Diogenes is pacified, but had he known that Mr. Toots was going to propose to Florence, he might actually have chased the suitor off to save her the pain of refusing him.

When Susan Nipper had to leave, as a consequence of speaking her mind to the mighty Mr. Dombey himself, Diogenes shared his mistress' grief at the parting and was seen to "bound after the cab, and want to follow and testify an impossibility of conviction that he had no longer any property in the fare." But the departure of Susan could be borne, while the departure of Florence could not. After the disappearance of Edith and the blow she received from her frenzied father when she offered him her sympathy, Florence could not stand life in the great house any longer. She fled from it into the streets, stunned and horrified and shamed. It was early morning, and she was alone. But a shadow darted past her, wheeled around, came close, and bounded round her. It was Diogenes, who refused to leave his young mistress in any circumstances. "Oh, Di," Florence exclaimed, "Oh, dear, true, faithful Di, how did you come here! How could I ever leave you, Di, who would never leave me?" Florence, in her distress, was filled with gratitude for the love of the dog; and as to him, we read:

"Di, more off the ground than on it, endeavouring to kiss his mistress, flying, tumbling over and getting up again without the least concern, dashing at big dogs in a jocose defiance of his species, terrifying with touches of his nose young housemaids who were cleaning doorsteps, and continually stopping in the midst of a thousand extravagances, to look back at Florence, and bark until all the dogs within hearing answered, and all the dogs who could come out, came out to stare at him."

Florence and Diogenes reach the home of Walter's uncle, of which Captain Cuttle is now in possession, and the worn out girl faints in the arms of the embarrassed seaman. The Captain does all within his power to revive and cheer her. Diogenes, meanwhile, has been looking at Cuttle trying to make up his mind whether to fly at him or offer him his friendship, "and he had expressed that conflict of feeling by alternate waggings of his tail, and displays of his teeth, with now and then a growl or so." But Diogenes finds in the Captain's favour and decides that he is "one of the most amiable of men" and one whom it is "an honour to a dog to know."

Florence is unable to eat anything owing to her distress, and Diogenes delays his supper to bark furiously at someone he supposes to be on the other side of the closed door of Gill's shop. This display all but reveals the presence of Florence to Mr. Toots, who pays a surprise call. Captain Cuttle evades the questions about the barking, but as Diogenes, who is upstairs guarding his mistress, might take it into his head to enter the parlour, he is relieved to see the back of his visitor with his secret still safe. Later, however, Mr. Toots learned all about Florence's presence in the house, and in his delight kissed her hand so fervently, fell on one knee, shed tears, and chuckled, that he ran the risk of a violent assault from Diogenes, who was quite unable to believe that these demonstrations were friendly, until a word from his mistress settled the doubt in his mind.

Diogenes settles down in his new home, and when Susan Nipper arrives he licks her face in his delight at seeing this old friend again. He is on very good terms with Captain Cuttle, but one evening he appeared rather uneasy.

" Diogenes was listening, and occasionally breaking out into a gruff, half-smothered fragment of a bark, of which he afterwards seemed half ashamed, as if he doubted having any reason for it.

"'Steady, steady!' said the Captain to Diogenes, 'what's amiss with you? You don't seem easy in your mind to-night, my boy.'

"Diogenes wagged his tail, but pricked up his ears immediately afterwards, and gave utterance to another fragment of a bark; for which he apologized to the Captain, by again wagging his tail."

The uneasiness of Diogenes is soon explained, for it is occasioned by the astonishing return of Sol Gills, who was believed to be dead.

Through the happy times which come to Florence with her marriage to Walter and the relenting of her father, Diogenes' fidelity never wavers; and the last picture of him is of an old dog in the happy company of the white-haired Dombey, now so changed, and the little boy and girl, his grandchildren.

Diogenes was very far from being a wonderful dog. He had not the sagacity of Bull's-eye, and his creator describes him as ridiculous. But in his love and faithfulness for Florence, and her gratitude for his companionship in her great loneliness, there is a very beautiful picture of the deep affection that often springs up between kindly men and women and their dumb pets. There is no doubt that but for Diogenes, Florence Dombey would have found life insupportable, and a tragedy might have occurred instead of the happy ending, which this humorous dog played an important part in bringing about.

BOXER

In Boxer from "The Cricket on the Hearth" we have what is, perhaps, the most delightful of all the dog characters of Dickens. His unfailing good humour, his affectionate nature, his sagacity, and his desire to make himself useful, constitute him just the pet to complete the beautiful picture of the harmonious home of the Peerybingles. Boxer was known to everybody and shared the general popularity of his master and mistress. He accompanied John Peerybingle on his rounds as a carrier, and had always a hearty greeting for friends of the family.

"Boxer gave occasion to more good-natured recognitions of and by the Carrier than half-a-dozen Christians could have done! Everybody knew him, all along the road. . . . He had business everywhere; going down all the turnings, looking into all the wells, bolting in and out of all the cottages, dashing into the midst of all the Dame-Schools, fluttering all the pigeons, magnifying the tails of all the cats, and trotting into the public-houses like a regular customer. Wherever he went, somebody or other might have been heard to cry, 'Halloa! Here's Boxer!' and out came that somebody forthwith, accompanied by at least two or three other somebodies, to give John Peerybingle and his pretty wife, Good Day."

The joy of life belonged to Boxer. He imbibed the cheerful atmosphere of his home and seemed to radiate good fellowship. He felt that "his attentions were due to the family in general, and must be impartially distributed." He wanted everybody to be happy, and saw to it that it was not his fault if they were not. Dickens pictures the dog:

"now describing a circle of short-barks round the horse, where he was being rubbed down at the stable-door; now feigning to make savage rushes at his mistress, and facetiously bringing himself to sudden stops; now eliciting a shriek from Tilly Slowboy, in the low nursing-chair near the fire, by the unexpected application of his moist nose to her countenance; now exhibiting an obtrusive interest in the Baby; now going round and round upon the hearth, and lying down as if he had established himself for the night; now getting up again, and taking that nothing of a fag-end of a tail of his, into the weather, as if he had just remembered an appointment, and was off, at a round trot, to keep it."

John Peerybingle, on his return home in the evening, had given a lift to an old gentleman, who had fallen asleep in the back of his cart. The slow but honest carrier had completely forgotten the stranger on arrival at his house, but Boxer was not so absent-minded. He kept a watchful eye upon him "lest he should walk off with a few young poplar trees that were tied up behind the cart." When the stranger entered the cottage, Boxer was still in close attendance, very conscious of his responsibilities, and worrying his gaiters to make it clear that he would stand no nonsense. The old gentleman, however, was not at all afraid of Boxer, probably because he intended no harm against his master and mistress, and because he was really a young gentleman disguised as an old one.

The wonderful instinct of Boxer was best shown in his treatment of the blind Bertha, the daughter of Caleb Plummer. The Peerybingles would often visit the toy-maker's home, and Boxer would run ahead, reach the door, and give notice of his master's and mistress' approach, so that Caleb and the blind girl were always waiting on the pavement to give them welcome.

"Boxer . . . made certain delicate distinctions of his own, in his communication with Bertha, which persuade me fully that he knew her to be blind. He never sought to attract her attention by looking at her, as he often did with other people, but touched her invariably. What experience he could ever have had of blind people or blind dogs, I don't know. He had never lived with a blind master; nor had Mr. Boxer the elder, nor Mrs. Boxer, nor any of his respectable family on either side, ever been visited with blindness, that I am aware of. He may have found it out for himself, perhaps, but he had got hold of it somehow; and therefore he had hold of Bertha, too, by the skirt, and kept hold, until . . . all got safely within doors."

An amusing request made by Caleb to Dot Peerybingle had reference to Boxer. He asked permission to pinch his tail for half a moment. He explained that a small order for barking dogs had come in and he wanted to get as near nature in his toys as possible. Boxer, without having his tail pinched, began to bark furiously, but as this was warning of the approach of a visitor, Caleb postponed "his study from life to a more convenient season."

When the gloom of a misunderstanding arose between John Peerybingle and his wife, Dot, Boxer's spirits did not droop, but he barked "as triumphantly and merrily as ever." When, again, all these difficulties were cleared away and happiness and confidence returned, "there wanted but one living creature to make the party complete," the party of reunited friends and lovers and reconciled enemies. This one was Boxer.

"And, in the twinkling of an eye, there he was: very thirsty with hard running. . . . He had gone with the cart to its journey's end, very much disgusted with the absence of his master, and stupendously rebellious to the Deputy. After lingering about the stable for some little time, vainly attempting to incite the old horse to the mutinous act of returning on his own account, he had walked into the tap room and laid himself down before the fire. But suddenly yielding to the conviction that the Deputy was a humbug, and must be abandoned, he had got up again, turned tail, and come home."

It is not possible to imagine the delightful story

of "The Cricket on the Hearth" without Boxer. He typifies the cheerful atmosphere and deep affection which surrounds the Peerybingles. Moreover, he carries it on while his master and mistress pass through the dark cloud of tears and suspicion, and in the end he is necessary to complete the picture of restoration to perfect happiness. Boxer is as lovable a dog as can be imagined, always so cheerful and good-natured. His wonderful sagacity in his treatment of the blind girl may appear a little exaggerated, but to those who are fond of dogs and have observed them closely, as Dickens must have done, it does not appear at all impossible, so extraordinary is canine intelligence.

JIP

Jip—short for Gypsy—was Dora Spenlow's little spaniel dog, whose acquaintance David Copperfield made on the occasion of his first visit to the home of his future wife. He was the constant companion of the fragile girl, and it is impossible to conjure up a mental picture of David's first love without including Jip. In appearance he was, it seems, small. "Jip remained to bark injuriously at an immense butcher's dog in the street, who could have taken him like a pill," is one reference to his size; while Dora's action in lifting him to smell the flowers shows that he was just the little lap dog that we should expect a girl of Dora's temperament and physique to have as her friend.

David, having fallen desperately in love with Jip's mistress, was prepared to love the dog for her sake. Jip, however, was not disposed to be friendly. He showed his teeth, snarled, and "wouldn't hear of the least familiarity." The truth was that he was jealous of David, and the jealous feeling appears to have been reciprocated.

"He was mortally jealous of me, and persisted in barking at me. She took him up in her arms—oh my goodness!—and caressed him, but he insisted upon barking still. He wouldn't let me touch him, when I tried; and then she beat him. It increased my sufferings greatly to see the pats she gave him for punishment on the bridge of his blunt nose, while he winked his eyes, and licked her hand, and still growled within himself like a little double-bass."

Perhaps David can be excused for his envy of Jip, for Dora would whisper her secrets into his ear and regard him as her confidential friend and protector. In reference to Miss Murdstone, whom Mr. Spenlow had engaged as her companion, she said:

"Jip can protect me a great deal better than Miss Murdstone — can't you, Jip, dear? . . . We are not going to confide in any such cross people, Jip and I. We mean to bestow our confidence where we like, and to find out our own friends, instead of having them found out for us —don't we, Jip?"

To these questions Jip answered in a comfortable manner, "like a tea-kettle when it sings," while David was more enslaved than ever by love for Dora.

David went again to the Spenlows home at Norwood, on the occasion of Dora's birthday, at her father's invitation. He rose early and was at Covent Garden at six in the morning, buying a bouquet for his love. On arrival at the house he found Jip with Dora, and the dog's attitude towards him was not improved. He was still jealous, and refused to give him his friendship.

"Jip was there, and Jip *would* bark at me again. When I presented my bouquet, he gnashed his teeth with jealousy. Well he might.

If he had the least idea how I adored his mistress, well he might."

Dora was delighted with David's present, and her friend, Julia Mills, whom the young man met for the first time, was greatly interested in the obvious fascination which had been cast over him. She herself had been unfortunate in her tender experiences, but was still able to sympathize with the unblighted hopes of others at the comparatively advanced age of twenty years!

Jip was apparently very angry about David's gift of flowers, and showed his displeasure.

" Dora held my flowers to Jip to smell. Then Jip growled, and wouldn't smell them. Then Dora laughed, and held them a little closer to Jip, to make him. Then Jip laid hold of a bit of geranium with his teeth, and worried imaginary cats with it. Then Dora beat him, and pouted, and said, 'My poor beautiful flowers!' as compassionately, I thought, as if Jip had laid hold of me. I wished he had!"

A better mood, however, came in time over Jip, and his jealousy for David Copperfield gave way to a kinder feeling. He realized that there was something serious between his mistress and the young man, something which was beyond his power to stop. David says: "Jip began to see how it was, and to understand that he must make up his mind to be friends with me." When the great moment came and David took Dora in his arms and poured his tale of love into her ear, Jip was there, and in his excitement "barked madly all the time." David became more and more eloquent, and, describing the scene, writes: "The more I raved, the more Jip barked. Each of us, in his own way, got more mad every moment." When the storm of passion had passed, and the calm and happiness which follows a love confessed and accepted had fallen upon them, the two sat quietly on the sofa, while Jip lay peacefully in Dora's lap, winking lazily at David.

As David told Dora that she had engaged herself to a poor man, Jip was there again, listening to the conversation. He had the utmost difficulty in persuading her to accept the truth and face the facts. Dora was not at all practical. She hated the word and considered it disagreeable. She threatened David with the only weapon at hand—Jip—if he talked on such unpleasant a subject as being poor.

"'Dora, my own dearest!' said I. 'I am a beggar!'

"'How can you be such a silly thing,' replied Dora, slapping my hand, 'as to sit there, telling such stories? I'll make Jip bite you. . . .'

"I solemnly repeated: 'Dora, my own life, I am your ruined David.'

"'I declare I'll make Jip bite you!' said Dora, shaking her curls, 'if you are so ridiculous.'"

But the situation was a serious one, and David's gravity convinced Dora that he was in earnest. Still, she did not want to hear about the distasteful things of life, but only the sweet.

"'Don't talk about being poor, and working hard!' said Dora, nestling closer to me. 'Oh, don't, don't.'

"'My dearest love,' said I, 'The crust well-earned——'

"'Oh, yes; but I don't want to hear any more about crusts!' said Dora. 'And Jip must have a mutton chop every day at twelve, or he'll die.'"

Dora tried to put an end to the conversation by begging David to kiss Jip and be agreeable, but he persisted, and the request to his love to study the cookery book produced a crisis, which was only passed by the timely arrival and help of Miss Mills.

David was soon to hear of action on the part of Jip which was to have very serious consequences.

One morning, on meeting Mr. Spenlow, he found that his greeting was not returned with the usual affability. Dora's father was cold and distant, and when he asked David to accompany him to a small coffee-shop in the vicinity for the obvious purpose of private conversation, the young lover was filled with apprehension that his secret love affair had been discovered. They proceeded to an upstair room, and any lingering hopes to which David may have clung were dashed to the ground by the discovery of the presence of Miss Murdstone.

Without wasting time over preliminaries Mr. Spenlow requested Miss Murdstone to show David Copperfield what she had in her reticule, and the embarrassed young man was confronted with the last of his affectionate and sentimental love-letters to Dora. This was followed by a whole parcel of his effusions, and David was compelled to acknowledge that they were in his handwriting. Mr. Spenlow thereupon requested Miss Murdstone to tell the story of this unfortunate discovery. The companion began by relating the suspicions that she had entertained respecting David and Dora from their first meeting. But suspicion without proof was not enough reason for speaking to Spenlow on the subject, and she set herself to watch, in the hope that she might obtain confirmation. It was Jip who betrayed the secret to "this dragon."

"'Last evening after tea,' pursued Miss Murdstone, 'I observed the little dog starting, rolling, and growling about the drawing-room, worrying something. I said to Miss Spenlow, "What is that the dog has in its mouth? It's paper." Miss Spenlow immediately put her hand to her frock, gave a sudden cry, and ran to the dog. I interposed, and said, "Dora, my love, you must permit me."'

"Oh, Jip, miserable spaniel, this wretchedness, then, was your work!

"'Miss Spenlow endeavoured,' said Miss Murdstone, 'to bribe me with kisses, workboxes, and small articles of jewellery—that, of course, I pass over. The little dog retreated under the sofa on my approaching him, and was with great difficulty dislodged by the fire-irons. Even when dislodged, he still kept the letter in his mouth; and on my endeavouring to take it from him, at the imminent risk of being bitten, he kept it between his teeth so pertinaciously as to suffer himself to remain suspended in the air by means of the document. At length I obtained possession of it. After perusing it I taxed Miss Spenlow with having many such letters in her possession: and ultimately obtained from her the packet which is now in David Copperfield's hand.'"

David had no very kind thoughts towards Jip for this betrayal, in spite of the fact that the little spaniel seemed reluctant enough to deliver the evidence into Miss Murdstone's hand. The revelation led to Mr. Spenlow forbidding Copperfield to have anything more to do with Dora, and the course of true love seemed to be running anything but smoothly. The sudden death of Spenlow, soon after the meeting in the coffee-shop, led to Dora moving to the home of her maiden aunts in Putney, whither Jip accompanied her. David receives news of his beloved through Miss Mills, who keeps a diary and sends him extracts for his information. One of these contains an account of an adventure of Jip's, who was stolen.

"'Man appears in kitchen, with blue bag, "for lady's boots left out to heel." Cook replies, " No such orders." Man argues point. Cook withdraws to enquire, leaving man alone with J. [Jip]. On Cook's return, man still argues point, but ultimately goes. J. missing. D. distracted. Information sent to police. . . . No J. D. weeping bitterly, and inconsolable. . . . Towards evening strange boy calls. Brought into parlour . . . says he wants a pound and knows a dog. Declines to explain further, though much pressed. Pound being produced by D., takes Cook to little house, where J. alone tied up to leg of table. Joy of D., who dances round J. while he eats his supper.'"

This experience does not appear to have left any permanent effect upon Jip, for when David receives permission from Dora's aunts to visit her in her new home, the dog is still occupying his usual place in the picture. He takes a great dislike, however, to David Copperfield's aunt—" All kinds of treatment were tried on him, coaxing, scolding, slapping . . . but he never could prevail upon himself to bear my Aunt's society." On the other hand, he responded instantly to the overtures of the gentle Agnes, and quickly made friends with her.

The time of David and Dora's wedding drew near, and the latter asked her pet to forgive her for getting married. Much is done to appease him, and he receives a present of a Chinese house, with little bells on the top, which is very nice for Jip, but much too large for their establishment. Jip attends the wedding, where he eats some of the cake, which disagrees with him, and afterwards accompanies the happy pair on their honeymoon. David has recollections:

"Of my wanting to carry Jip (who is to go along with us) and Dora's saying No, that she must carry him, or else he'll think she don't like him any more, now she is married, and will break his heart."

Jip found no difficulty in settling down quickly in the new home. In David's eye he was less perfect than he was in that of Dora. The young husband somewhat disapproved of his walking on the tablecloth during meal times, his habit of putting his foot in the salt, and his barking and running at the guests, which monopolized the attention and conversation of the company. He also disapproved of Jip's annoying manner of spoiling all Dora's efforts at keeping the weekly accounts.

"When she had entered two or three laborious items in the account-book, Jip would walk over the page, wagging his tail, and smear them all out. . . . Then she would call Jip up to look at his misdeeds."

But Jip was necessary to Dora's happiness, and David was kind and tolerant towards him for her sake. He even brought him a new collar, when he wanted to be particularly nice and agreeable to his wife.

Illness lays its hand on Dora, and one of the most moving passages in "David Copperfield" is the young girl's realization that her playmate Jip is growing old. David's aunt endeavours to speak cheerfully of the spaniel's future, but she cannot hide the fact that he is asthmatical and unable to run about as he used. She tries to console Dora, by promising to give her another dog, if anything should happen to Jip, but the girl answers:

"I couldn't have any other dog but Jip. . . . It would be so unkind to Jip! Besides, I couldn't be such friends with any other dog, but Jip; because he wouldn't have known me before I was married, and wouldn't have barked at Doady when he first came to our house. I couldn't care for any other dog but Jip, I am afraid."

Dora grows worse and worse, and David realizes that never again will he see his little wife running about with her companion Jip. The latter seems to the sorrowful young husband to have aged as Dora has grown worse.

"He is, as it were suddenly, grown very old. It may be, that he misses in his mistress something that enlivened him and made him younger; but he mopes, and his sight is weak, and his limbs are feeble, and my aunt is sorry that he objects to her no more, but . . . mildly licks her hand."

The sands of Dora's young life are quickly running out, and the moment is reached when the little heart becomes still. David is in the parlour alone with Jip, and Agnes has gone to the dying girl. Jip is lying in his Chinese house by the fire, but he is restless, and crawls out, wanders to the door, and whines to go up to his mistress.

" 'Not to-night, Jip! Not to-night.' He comes very slowly back to me, licks my hand, and lifts his dim eyes to my face.
" ' Oh, Jip. It may be, never again!'
" He lies down at my feet, stretches himself out as if to sleep, and with a plaintive cry, is dead."

Agnes appears at that moment to tell David that all is over. Jip and his mistress have died together.

Such is the story of the little pet of Dora Spenlow. We cannot say that Jip was in any way a remarkable dog. He had no greatly developed instincts nor marked sagacity. Even the tricks which Dora pretended to have taught him were not performed in very convincing style. Of his standing on his hind legs in a corner David said he did it "for about the space of a flash of lightning, and then fell down." Moreover, he was often extremely reluctant to go through his performances, and Dora was often compelled to let him off. Although Jip was a very ordinary dog, he has nevertheless a personality which is so much a part of the story of "David Copperfield," that the reader would be conscious of something important missing, were an edition printed with Jip omitted. He seems to be quite a part of Dora and serves the literary purpose of throwing light upon the young girl's character. The loyalty and affection of Jip for his mistress are as great as in any of Dickens' dumb animals, and it was a fitting end that he should pass with her through death to the mysteries beyond.

MERRYLEGS

Merrylegs was the trained performing dog of Signor Jupe, a clown in Sleary's circus in "Hard Times." Signor Jupe had a daughter Cecilia, who attended the school which was under the direction of Mr. Gradgrind. Mr. Bounderby held the idea that Cecilia had a bad influence over the other children, seeing that she was the child of a showman, and he and Mr. Gradgrind pay a visit to the Pegasus' Arms at Pod's End to inform Jupe that the privilege granted to his daughter must now be withdrawn.

On the way they meet Sissy (or Cecilia), who undertakes to conduct them to her father. She asks them to wait while she finds her parent, adding, "If you should hear a dog, sir, it's only Merrylegs, and he only barks." But they see no dog and no Signor Jupe, for the clown has fled, accompanied by Merrylegs. Jupe has grown too stiff in the joints to perform his parts, and, as he believes Sissy is safe in the school and well provided for, decides to disappear and remove any handicap that he may be to her. Faced with this unexpected situation Mr. Gradgrind determines to take charge of the girl and attend to her support and education.

Nothing is known of the fate of Signor Jupe, but a long, long time afterwards Merrylegs returned to Sleary, the proprietor of the circus, where he worked with his master. Sleary refers to the incident in a talk with Mr. Gradgrind about the wonderful instinct of dogs, and the occasion is the escape, with Sleary's help, of Mr. Gradgrind's son, who was in danger of arrest for the robbery of Bounderby's bank. In this escape a dog had played a principal part, and so led to general remarks upon the whole canine race.

"'Thquire, you don't need to be told that dogth ith wonderful animalth.'

"'Their instinct,' said Mr. Gradgrind, 'is surprising.'

"'Whatever you call it—and I'm bletht if I know what to call it,' said Sleary, 'it ith athtonithing the way in whith a dog'll find you— the dithtanthe he'll come.'

"'His scent,' said Mr. Gradgrind, 'being so fine.'

"'I'm bletht if I know what to call it,' repeated Sleary, shaking his head, 'but I have had dogth find me, Thquire, in a way that made me think whether that dog hadn't gone to another dog and thed: "You don't happen to know a Perthon of the name of Thleary in the Horthe-Riding way—thtout man—game eye?" And whether that dog mightn't have thed, "Well I can't thay I know him mythelf, but I know a dog that I think would be likely to be acquainted with him." And whether that dog mightn't have thought it over and thed, "Thleary, Thleary! Oh, yeth, to be thure. A friend of mine mentioned him to me at one time. I can get you hith addreth directly." ' "

Sleary's theory is that, being before the public with his horse-riding entertainment, a great number of dogs must be acquainted with him, who pass on information concerning him from one to another. In no other way can he account for the wonderful way in which Merrylegs traced him after many years' absence. Mr. Gradgrind is quite confounded by Sleary's idea, but he listens, nevertheless, to what he has to say.

" ' Anyway . . . ith fourteen month ago, Thquire, thinthe we wath at Chethter. We wath getting up our Children in the Wood one morning, when there cometh into our Ring, by the thtage door, a dog. He had travelled a long way; he wath in very bad condithon, he wath lame, and pretty well blind. He went round to our children, one after another, ath if he wath a-theeking for a child he know'd, and then he come to me, and throw'd hithelf up behind, and thtood on hith two fore-legth, weak ath he wath, and then he wagged hith tail and died. Thquire, that dog wath Merrylegth.' "

Mr. Gradgrind remembers the name as that of the dog of Sissy Jupe's father. Sleary confirms it and voices the opinion from his knowledge of Merrylegs, that he remained with his master until he was dead and buried before returning to him and the circus. Thus does the novelist make use of the canine instinct to clear up a point respecting the fate of one of his characters, but it is clear from the conversation that proceeds between Sleary and Mr. Gradgrind that he took the opportunity to emphasize in Merrylegs that canine instinct, which is ever astonishing and about which so little is really known.

POODLES

In the "Uncommercial Traveller" we have one of the most attractive of the dog characters of Dickens, who enjoys the name of Poodles. He appears in two of the New Uncommercial Samples, which were published in "All The Year Round" in 1869, namely, "A Small Star in the East" and "On An Amateur Beat."

From the former we learn something of the history of Poodles. He is a comical dog, who was found starving at the door of the East London Children's Hospital and taken in and fed. By this act of kindness he was persuaded to make the institution his home and soon became on familiar terms with all the patients. He enjoys great popularity and is described as "quite a tonic in himself." Round his neck he wears a collar given to him by "an admirer of his mental endowments," which bears the inscription, "Judge not Poodles by external appearances."

In "On An Amateur Beat" the traveller pays another visit to the Children's Hospital and improves his acquaintance with the inimitable Poodles. He finds the walls of the wards are profusely garnished with dolls, and wonders what is the opinion of Poodles about them. The dog, he discovers, has greater interest in the patients than the dolls in their splendid dresses, and describes him as follows:

"I find him making the round of the beds, like a house-surgeon, attended by another dog—a friend—who appears to trot about with him in the character of his pupil dresser. Poodles is anxious to make me known to a pretty little girl looking wonderfully healthy, who has had a leg taken off for cancer of the knee. 'A difficult operation,' Poodles intimates, wagging his tail on the counterpane, 'but perfectly successful, as you see, dear sir.' The patient, patting Poodles, adds, with a smile, 'The leg was so much trouble to me that I'm glad it's gone.' I never saw anything in doggery finer than the deportment of Poodles when another little girl opens her mouth to show a peculiar enlargement of the tongue. Poodles (at that time on a table, to be on a level with the occasion) looks at the tongue (with his own sympathetically out) so very gravely and knowingly, that I feel inclined to put my hand in my waistcoat pocket and give him a guinea, wrapped in paper."

There can be few pleasanter pictures of dog life in literature than that of Poodles, trotting among the beds of the Children's Hospital, talking to the patients, taking a sympathetic interest in their complaints, and encouraging them in their troubles.

The sample, "On An Amateur Beat," illustrates sagacity and affection for human beings on the part of dogs through the description of Poodles, but he is not the only dog referred to in this chapter. Another, showing canine inquisitiveness, as well as reasoning power, is mentioned. The traveller is pursuing his way near the Whitechapel Road, when he sees a doubled-up old woman plodding her weary journey. The sight is unusual in this part of the city, being more common in the Strand and thoroughfares adjacent thereto. That she is a strange spectacle is impressed upon the traveller by the action of a dog, "a lop-sided mongrel with a foolish tail," who, with his ears pricked, displays an "amiable interest in the ways of his fellow-men." The traveller describes thus the curiosity of the dog and his cautious explorations:

"After pausing at a porkshop, he is jogging eastward like myself, with a benevolent countenance and a watery mouth, as though musing on the many excellencies of pork, when he beholds this doubled-up bundle approaching. He is not so much astonished by the bundle (though amazed by that), as the circumstance that it has within itself the means of locomotion. He stops, pricks his ears higher, makes a slight point, stares, utters a short, low growl, and glistens at the nose—as I conceive with terror. The bundle continuing to approach, he barks, turns tail, and is about to fly, when, arguing with himself, that flight is not becoming in a dog, he turns and once more faces the advancing heap of clothes. After much hesitation, it occurs to him that there may be a face in it somewhere. Desperately resolving to undertake the adventure, and pursue the inquiry, he goes slowly up to the bundle, goes slowly round, and coming at length upon the human countenance, down there where never human countenance should be, gives a yelp of horror, and flies for the East India Docks."

The Uncommercial Traveller displays in these passages a very keen observation of the habits and manners of dogs. We are amused at the inquisitiveness of the unnamed animal and his reasoning powers, and we love the sympathetic and friendly qualities of the comical Poodles, who is representative of that type of dog ever the loyal and trusted companion of man.

SPORTING DOGS AND OTHERS

Dickens' knowledge of the canine world included an acquaintance with sporting dogs. The classic instance in which the novelist refers to these sagacious creatures, is Mr. Wardle's shooting party in "Pickwick," when Mr. Tupman unexpectedly distinguished himself by hitting a plump partridge, while Mr. Winkle, the pseudo-sportsman, covered himself with disgrace.

Mr. Wardle has a strong affection for his dumb friends.

"'Hi, Juno, lass—hi, old girl; down, Daph, down,' said Wardle, caressing the dogs."

He is much concerned for their safety during Mr. Winkle's erratic handling of his gun. We are told it was such "as to place the lives of the two dogs on a rather uncertain and precarious tenure."

Winkle betrays his complete lack of sporting knowledge and experience, and reveals the hollowness of his reputation as a sportsman when the dogs come to a dead stop, causing the party to halt also.

"'What's the matter with the dogs' legs?' whispered Mr. Winkle. 'How queer they're standing.'

"'Hush, can't you?' replied Wardle, softly. 'Don't you see they're making a point?'

"'Making a point!' said Mr. Winkle, staring about him, as if he expected to discover some particular beauty, which the sagacious animals were calling special attention to. 'Making a point! What are they pointing at?'"

Mr. Wardle is too excited to pay much attention to this absurd question. He bids Mr. Winkle keep his eyes open; and as the birds rise he bags a brace, which the well-trained dogs recover and deposit at his feet.

The most wonderful of all dogs, however, is Ponto, belonging to Mr. Alfred Jingle—so wonderful, indeed, that anyone but the credulous Mr. Pickwick would have seen that his cleverness existed chiefly in his owner's imagination. On the Rochester coach Jingle surveys Mr. Winkle's sporting disguise, and addresses him:

"'Sportsman, sir?' abruptly turning to Mr. Winkle.

"'A little, sir,' replied that gentleman.

"'Fine pursuit, sir — fine pursuit — Dogs, sir?'

"'Not just now,' said Mr. Winkle.

"'Ah! you should keep dogs—fine animals—sagacious creatures—dog of my own once—Pointer—surprising instinct—out shooting one day—entering inclosure—whistled—dog stopped—whistled again—Ponto—no go; stock still—called him—Ponto, Ponto—wouldn't move—dog transfixed—staring at a board—looked up, saw an inscription—"Gamekeeper has order to shoot all dogs found in this inclosure"—wouldn't pass it—wonderful dog—valuable dog that—very.'

"'Singular circumstance that,' said Mr. Pickwick. 'Will you allow me to make a note of it?'"

Mr. Jingle gives a courteous assent and assures the great man that he has a hundred more anecdotes of the wonderful Ponto!

Performing dogs are mentioned by Dickens in "The Old Curiosity Shop." The occasion is the arrival of Little Nell and her grandfather with their travelling companions, Thomas Codlin and Harris (alias Short Trotters), the showmen, at "The Jolly Sandboys" inn.

The company are disturbed by the sound of strange footsteps and the entry of new visitors.

"These were no other than four very dismal dogs, who came pattering in one after the other, headed by an old bandy dog of particularly mournful aspect, who, stopping when the last of his followers had got as far as the door, erected himself upon his hind legs and looked round at his companions, who immediately stood upon their hind legs in a grave and melancholy row. Nor was this the only remarkable circumstance about these dogs, for each of them wore a kind of little coat of some gaudy colour trimmed with tarnished spangles, and one of them had a cap upon his head, tied very carefully under his chin, which had fallen down upon his nose and completely obscured one eye. . . ."

The appearance of these dressed-up dogs, wet with rain and splashed with mud, did not surprise the showmen and the landlord. They merely heralded the approach of Jerry, who had won fame with his troop of canine dancers. The owner soon followed, and after cautioning one of his dogs named Pedro, who persisted in standing on his hind legs when there was no occasion, produced a little animal from a capacious pocket, who had once played the part of Toby in Codlin and Short Trotter's show. The little dog is so delighted at meeting his old masters that he has to be returned to the pocket for an excess of exuberance.

With the arrival of food the performing dogs became very excited, and started standing on their hind legs once more. Little Nell was about to throw a morsel to one of them, when Jerry stopped her. The dog had apparently disgraced himself at one performance by losing a halfpenny. His punishment was to go without supper; and he was compelled to play the Old Hundredth on his master's organ, while his companions fed. The sentence was severe, but discipline was rigid in Jerry's troop, and the handle of the instrument continued to revolve to the accompaniment of short howls of lament and protest from the hungry player.

Dogs trained to a grim duty are referred to by Dickens in "The Clock Case" in "Master Humphrey's Clock." These are bloodhounds used for the detection of crime. The story concerns a man who had served in the Army. He and his brother marry two sisters, but his brother's wife haunts him in a strange way. When she dies in childbirth, and is followed to the grave by her husband, the orphan is left with the ex-soldier and his wife. But in the child he sees the mother, and in a fit of frenzy murders him and buries him in the garden. When visitors call he places his chair over the spot and, feeling safer from detection, tries to drink and talk in a natural manner. Bloodhounds, who have escaped from their keeper, bound into the garden and start running to and fro, their noses on the ground, and sniffing eagerly. By and by they become keener still and keep to one spot.

"At last they came up close to the great chair on which I sat, and raising their frightful howl once more, tried to tear away the wooden rails that kept them from the ground beneath."

The action of the dogs, who are soon "tearing at the earth and throwing it up into the air like water," betrays the murderer and leads to his arrest. This dramatic story is his confession, made in gaol, while awaiting execution.

The foregoing extracts from the novelist's works throw still more light on his great knowledge of the dog, and show that all kinds and breeds had attracted his observant eye.

Just as Dickens invested each of his men and women with a distinctive personality, so that they have won immortal fame, in the same way he gave his dogs special traits of character of their own, so that they become individual and defined. He dealt with different sides of dog nature. In Bull's-eye we have a highly developed instinct and wonderful sagacity, but an uncertain temper, which, however, we can forgive in the circumstances. In Jip and Diogenes we have great devotion and loyalty to a particular human being, without any pronounced gifts of intelligence. In Boxer we have that refreshing good humour and joy of life, that friendliness and desire to help, which would make the world run more smoothly if there were more of it. In Merrylegs we have loyalty to his master and a wonderful instinct as the outstanding features, and in Poodles we have a sympathy and understanding that are almost human.

The creator of these outstanding dog characters, characters which, as we have seen, played a worthy part in the plots and were far from being merely ornamental additions, must have been keenly interested in the canine race. He must have observed dogs closely, for we can recognize in our own pets the amusing extravagances of Diogenes or Jip, and know how true to life they really are. It is consistent with the humanitarianism of Dickens that he should know how man may grow to love the dog, who is his best friend in the animal kingdom, and if we turn to the pages of Forster, his biographer, we find there the description of his own pets and his fondness for them, proving our deductions to be true.

Forster, in his pictures of the private life of the great novelist, says: "Dickens' interest in dogs (as in the habits and ways of all animals) was inexhaustible, and he welcomed with delight any new trait." He mentions the dog given to Dickens by Mr. Mitchell, the comedian, while the author was in America in 1842. This pet was christened Timber Doodle, afterwards changed to Snittle Timbery, "as more sonorous and expressive." Timber died at Boulogne in October 1855 to the great grief of Dickens.

At Gadshill Dickens had many dog companions. Forster writes: "His dogs were a great enjoyment to him. . . . There were always two, of the mastiff kind, but latterly the number increased." One of his favourites was Turk, who was killed by a railway accident, an incident that affected Dickens deeply. Turk's companion for a long time was Linda, a great St. Bernard. After Turk came Sultan, an Irish dog, who was so fierce and savage that he had to be killed. Dickens said that he must have been a Fenian from his habit of flying at anything in scarlet remotely resembling a British uniform. Sultan was succeeded by a grand Newfoundland named Don, who with Linda became the parent of two Newfoundland puppies, one of which was called Bumble, on account of "a peculiarly pompous and overbearing manner he had of appearing to mount guard over the yard when he was quite an infant."

Dickens wrote describing his joyous welcome home by the dogs on his return to Gadshill Place after his second visit to America. They were filled with delight at seeing him again, for they had missed accompanying him on his usual rambles. In 1865 Dickens was attacked by lameness and fell suddenly limp during a walk, with the result that he had to hobble home three miles through the snow. He tells of the consternation of Turk, who gave him such a look of sympathy and anxiety, and crept so close beside him, going as slowly as he, that the novelist was strangely moved. As for Linda, she was "wholly struck down" by his misfortune.

These glimpses of the novelist's experience with his own dogs explain that sympathy with, and understanding of, dog life, which are illustrated so wonderfully in the many canine characters in the novels of Dickens.